I0901245

Citified!

Mexico City

by Joyce Markovics

Consultant: Karla Ruiz, MA
Teachers College, Columbia University
New York, New York

BEARPORT PUBLISHING

New York, New York

Credits

Cover, © Kamira/Shutterstock; TOC Left, © studio BM/Shutterstock; TOC Right, © Chad Zuber/Shutterstock; 4–5, © Kamira/Shutterstock; 7, © Hashirama/Shutterstock; 8, © Carver Mostardi/Alamy Stock Photo; 9, © Alexcrab/iStock; 10–11, © Torresigner/iStock; 12, © Mardzpe/Dreamstime; 12BR, © Annmarie Young/Shutterstock; 13, © excentric_01/iStock; 14L, © Leonardo Emiliozzi/Shutterstock; 14R, © Byelikova Oksana/Shutterstock; 15, © migstock/Alamy Stock Photo; 16T, © Kevinwiel/Dreamstime; 16B, © Jesús Eloy Ramos Lara/Dreamstime; 17, © Patrick Rolands/Shutterstock; 18T, © bonchan/Shutterstock; 18B, © ProtoplasmaKid/CC BY-SA 4.0; 19, © Dolores Giraldez Alonso/Shutterstock; 20–21, © Kobby Dayan/Shutterstock; 22 (Clockwise from Top Right), © Noradoa/Shutterstock, © Aleksandar Todorovic/Shutterstock, © Marcelo Rodriguez/Shutterstock, © Leonardo Emiliozzi/Shutterstock, and © Jesús Eloy Ramos Lara/Dreamstime; 23 (T to B), © steve estvanik/Shutterstock, © Vincent St. Thomas/Shutterstock, © posztos/Shutterstock, © Aleksandar Todorovic/Shutterstock, and © posztos/Shutterstock; 24, © Aleksandar Todorovic/Shutterstock.

Publisher: Kenn Goin
Senior Editor: Joyce Tavolacci
Creative Director: Spencer Brinker
Photo Researcher: Thomas Persano

Library of Congress Cataloging-in-Publication Data

Names: Markovics, Joyce L., author.
Title: Mexico City / by Joyce Markovics.
Description: New York, New York : Bearport Publishing 2018. | Series: Citified! | Includes bibliographical references and index.
Identifiers: LCCN 2017005118 (print) | LCCN 2017017203 (ebook) | ISBN 9781684022908 (ebook) | ISBN 9781684022366 (library)
Subjects: LCSH: Mexico City (Mexico)—Juvenile literature.
Classification: LCC F1386 (ebook) | LCC F1386 .M35 2018 (print) | DDC 972/.53—dc23
LC record available at https://lccn.loc.gov/2017005118

For more information, write to Bearport Publishing Company, Inc., 45 West 21st Street, Suite 3B, New York, New York 10010. Printed in the United States of America.

10 9 8 7 6 5 4 3 2 1

Contents

Welcome to MEXICO CITY

The City of Palaces!

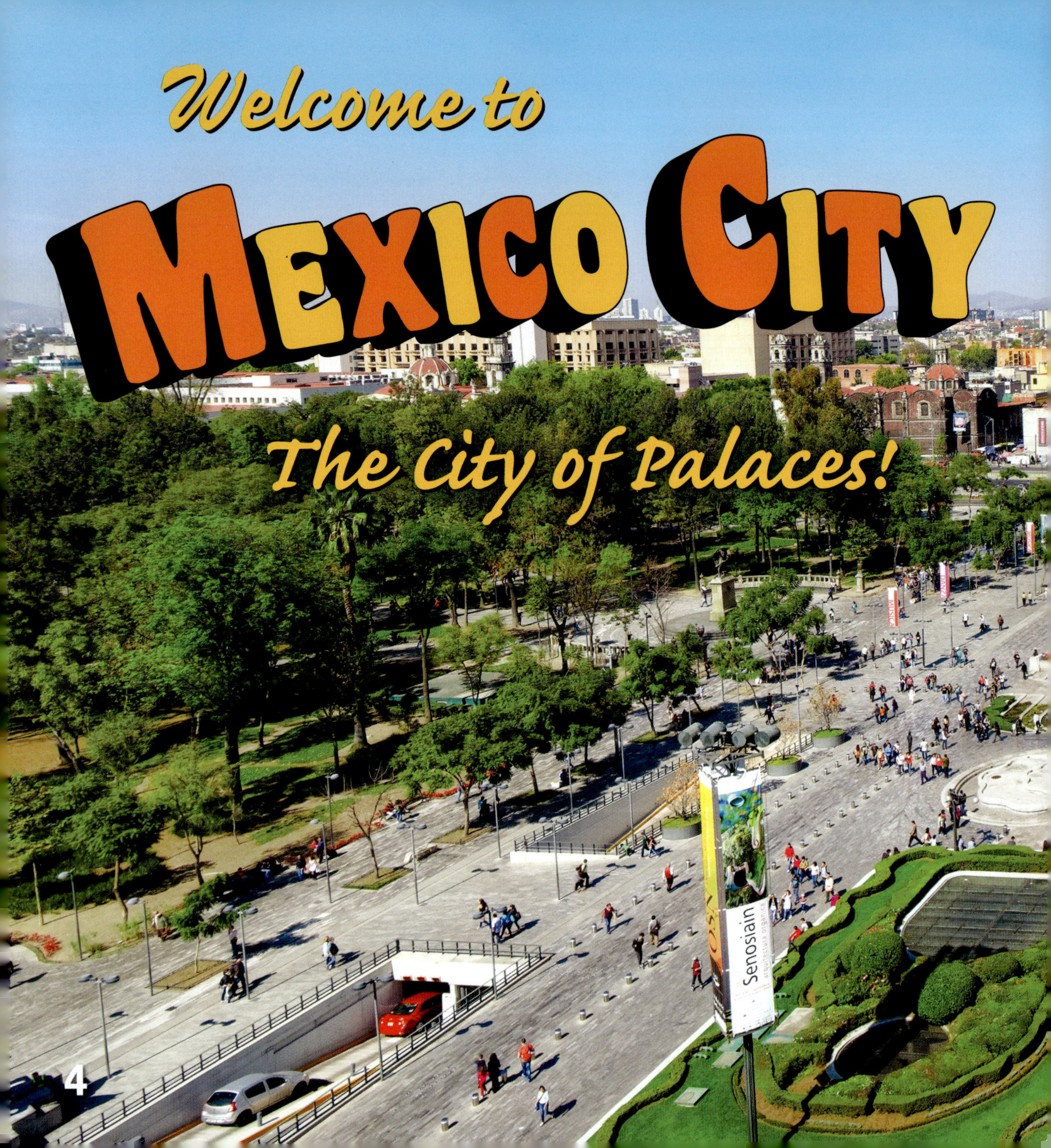

Mexico City was founded in 1521.

Mexico City is the biggest city in North America!

Almost nine million people live there.

Mexico City is also the **capital** of Mexico.

The city dates back thousands of years.

It was built on land that used to be under a giant lake.

Today, Mexico City is sinking.

Each year, the soggy land drops about 4 inches (10 cm)!

There's a huge **cathedral** in Mexico City. It's sinking, too! The church's floors are sloped.

People gather at the Zócalo.

It's a giant **public** square in the heart of the city.

Grand buildings and palaces line the square.

The Zócalo is one of the largest public squares in the world!

One part of Mexico City is filled with **canals**.

The area is known as Xochimilco (soh-chee-MEEL-koh).

It means “place of the flowers.”

Here, people grow flowers on floating platforms.

Visitors view the floating gardens from colorful boats.

Flying high above the city's Chapultepec (chah-PUHL-tee-pek) Park are *voladores*.

One man sits at the top of a tall pole.

Four other men who are tied to the pole jump off the top.

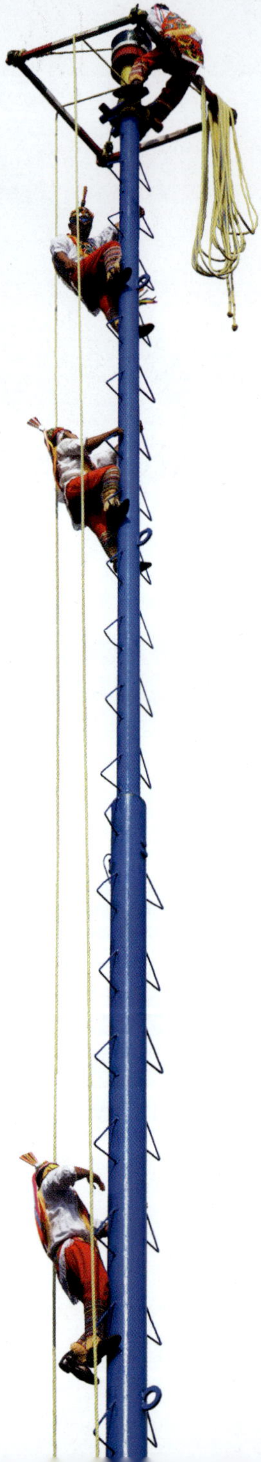

Then they soar around it!

Pole flying in Mexico dates back thousands of years. It was believed to help bring rain.

What else is wonderful about Mexico City?

The Chapultepec Zoo!

Visit its white tigers and tall giraffes.

The zoo houses 2,000 animals!

See its rare
thick-billed
parrots.

Mexico City is famous for its street food.

Grilled corn called *elote* (ay-LOW-tay) is a special treat.

People also enjoy tacos and cheesy *tlacoyos* (tla-COY-yoz).

Hot chocolate and fried dough called *churros* are popular for breakfast.

Mariachi (mahr-ee-AH-chee) bands play for **tourists**.

People enjoy the lively music.

Each year, more than 29 million visitors come to Mexico City!

Mariachi is a kind of Mexican folk music.

MAP IT!

Mexico City

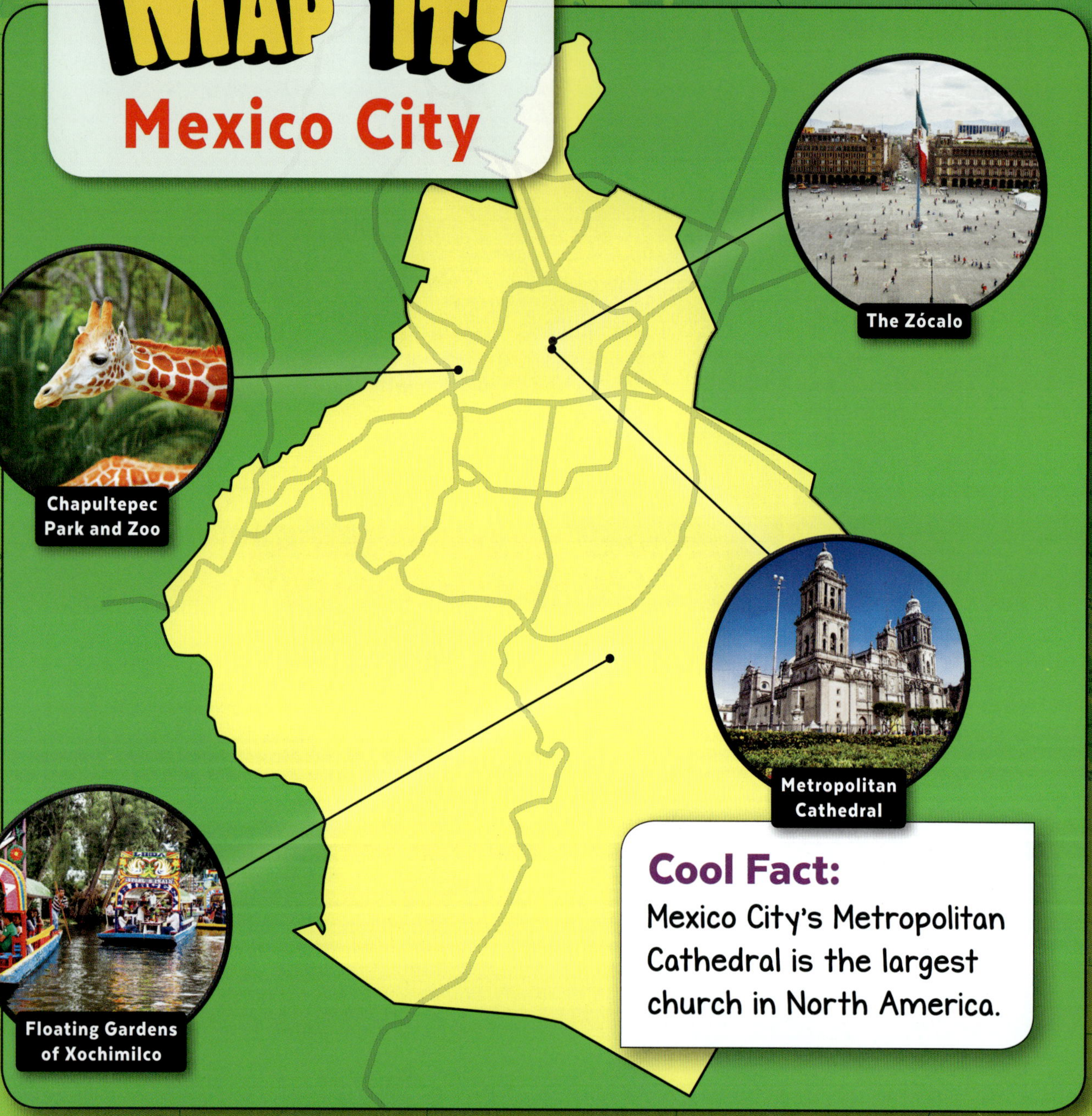

Cool Fact:

Mexico City's Metropolitan Cathedral is the largest church in North America.

Glossary

canals (kuh-NALZ) human-made waterways

capital (KAP-uh-tuhl) a city where a country's government is based

cathedral (kuh-THEE-druhl) a large, important church

public (PUHB-lik) open to or shared by all people in a community

tourists (TOOR-ists) people who travel and visit places for pleasure

Index

Read More

Perkins, Chloe. *Living in . . . Mexico (Ready-to-Read).* New York: Simon Spotlight (2016).

Sexton, Colleen. *Mexico (Blastoff! Readers: Exploring Countries).* Minnetonka, MN: Bellwether (2010).

Learn More Online

To learn more about Mexico City, visit
www.bearportpublishing.com/Citified

About the Author

Joyce Markovics lives along the Hudson River in a very old house. She has never been to Mexico but would love to tour the entire country one day.